Morse, Samuel Finley Breese, 1791-1872.

Imminent dangers to the free institutions of the United States

The American
Immigration Collection

Imminent Dangers to the Free Institutions of the United States Through Foreign Immigration

SAMUEL F. B. MORSE

Arno Press and The New York Times

NEW YORK 1969

*

Library of Congress Catalog Card No. 69-18785

*

Reprinted from a copy in the
University of Michigan Libraries

*

Manufactured in the United States of America

IMMINENT DANGERS

TO THE

FREE INSTITUTIONS OF THE UNITED STATES

THROUGH

FOREIGN IMMIGRATION,

AND THE PRESENT STATE

OF THE

NATURALIZATION LAWS.

A SERIES OF NUMBERS

ORIGINALLY PUBLISHED IN THE NEW-YORK JOURNAL OF COMMERCE.

BY

AN AMERICAN.

REVISED AND CORRECTED, WITH ADDITIONS

"To [the principles of our government,] nothing can be more opposed than the maxims of *absolute monarchies.* Yet from such we are to expect the greatest number of *emigrants.* They will bring with them *the principles* of the governments they lêave, *imbibed in their early youth; * * * * In proportion to their numbers *they will share with us the legislation.* They will infuse into it *their spirit, warp* and *bias its directions,* and render it a *heterogeneous, incoherent, distracted mass.* * * * *I doubt the expediency of inviting them* by extraordinary encouragements."—JEFFERSON. *Notes on Virginia.*

NEW-YORK:

E. B. CLAYTON, PRINTER, 17 HANOVER-STREET.

1835.

PREFACE.

It is but too common a remark of late, that the American character has within a short time been sadly degraded by numerous instances of riot and lawless violence in action, and a dangerous spirit of licentiousness in discussion. While these facts are universally acknowledged, the surprise is as universal that this degeneracy should exist, and the attempts to explain the mystery are various and contradictory. There are some who rashly attribute it to the natural tendency of Democracy, which they say is essentially turbulent. This is the most dangerous opinion of any that is advanced, as it must of necessity weaken the attachment of those who advance it, to our form of government, and must produce in them a criminal indifference to its policy, or traitorous desires for its overthrow.—Despotism often displays to shallow observers the exterior of justice on the part of the ruler, and the outside show of order and contentment on the part of the ruled. Yet look beneath the surface, and injustice, it will be seen, usually usurps the throne, and covers its oppressive decrees in mystery and darkness; while the oppressed people, restrained from complaint by physical force, are compelled to endure in silence, and smile while they suffer. *Despotism* is rank *hypocrisy.*—Democracy is, at least, no hypocrite,—it is honest and frank; and if there are occasions when its waywardness and folly offend, yet its whole character is open to view, and its irregularities can be checked and radically cured by enlightened public opinion. How much better, to be occasionally pained at the unsightly eruptions which often in the highest health of the body deform the surface, than to glory in that beautiful and lustrous complexion and hectic glow, the symptoms of organic disease, and the sure precursors of a sudden dissolution.

I cannot adopt the opinion, either that Democracies are naturally turbulent, or that the American character has suddenly undergone a radical change from good to bad; from that of habitual reverence for the laws, to that of riot and excess. It is not in the ordinary course of things, that the character of nations, any more than of individuals, change suddenly.

When the activity of benevolence, in every shape, which has been so long at work, through the length and breadth of our land, is considered, we naturally look for a corresponding result upon our society, in a more elevated moral character, and greater intellectual improvement, more love of moral truth, and regard for social order. To a slight observer, however, a result the very reverse seems to have been the consequence. I say it *seems* thus to a *slight observer:* to one who looks more deeply, a solid substratum of sound moral principle will appear to be evidently laid, while the surface alone presents to our view this moral paradox. How can it be explained?

If there is nothing *intrinsic* in our society which is likely to produce so sudden and mysterious an effect, the inquiry is natural, are there not *extrinsic* causes at work which have operated to disturb the harmonious movements of our system?

Here is a field we have not explored. We have not taken into the account all, or even the principal adverse causes which affect our government from without. One great opposing cause that embarrasses the benevolent operations of the country has apparently been wholly left out of the calculation, and yet it is a cause, which, more than all others, one would think, ought first to have attracted attention. This cause is FOREIGN IMMIGRATION. It is impossible in the nature of things that the moral character, and condition of this population, and its immense and alarming increase within a few years, should not have produced a counteracting effect on the benevolent operations of the day. How is it possible that foreign turbulence imported by ship-loads, that riot and ignorance in hundreds of thousands of human priest-controlled machines, should suddenly be thrown into our society, and not produce here turbulence and excess? Can one throw mud into pure water and not disturb its clearness?

There are other causes of a deeply serious nature, giving *support*, and *strength*, and *systematic operation*, to all these *adverse* effects of *foreign immigration*, and to which it is high time every American should seriously turn his thoughts. Some of these causes are exposed in the following numbers.

New-York, August, 1835. AN AMERICAN.

IMMINENT DANGERS

TO THE FREE INSTITUTIONS OF THE UNITED STATES THROUGH

FOREIGN IMMIGRATION,

AND THE

Present State of the Naturalization Laws.

No. I.

INTRODUCTORY REMARKS.

THE great question regarding Foreigners, and a change in our Naturalization laws, is a *National question*, and at this time a very serious one. It is therefore with deep regret that I perceive an attempt made by both parties, (however to be expected,) to turn the just National excitement on this subject each to the account of their own party. The question, *Whether Foreigners shall be subjected to a new law of naturalization?* which grave circumstances have recently made it necessary to examine, is one entirely separate at present from *party* politics, as parties are now constituted, and is capable of being decided solely on its own merits. The organs of the two parties, however, are noticing the subject, and both engaged in their usual style of recrimination. Neither of them can see the other, nor any measure however separated from party principle, if proposed or discussed by its opponent, except through the distorted medium of prejudice. So degraded in this particular has the party press become, in the view of the intelligent portion of the community, that no one seems to expect impartiality or independence, when any question is debated that affects, or even but seems to affect, the slightest change in the aspect of the party, or in the standing of the individual, whose cause it advocates. The exclusive party character of a great portion of the daily press, its distortion of facts, its gross vituperative tone and spirit, its defence of dangerous practices and abuses, if any of these but temporarily favour mere party designs, is a serious cause of alarm to the American people. To increase the evil, each party adopts the unlawful weapons of warfare of its antagonist, thinking it an ample justification of its conduct, if it can but show that they have been used by its opponent. I cannot but advert to this crying evil at a moment when a great and pressing danger to the country demands the attention of Americans of all parties, and their cool and dispassionate examination of the evidence in the case.

The danger to which I would call attention is not imaginary. It is a danger arising from *a new position of the social elements in the onward march of the world to liberty.* The great struggle for some years has till now been principally confined to Europe. But we cannot exclude, if we would, the influence of foreign movements upon our own political institutions, in the great contest between liberty and despotism. It is an ignorance unaccountable in the conductors of the press at this moment, not to know, and a neglect of duty unpardonable, not to guard the people against the dangers resulting from this source. To deny the danger, is to shut one's eyes. It stares us in the face. And to seek to allay the salutary alarm arising from a demonstration of its actual presence among us, by attributing this alarm to any but the right cause, is worse than folly, it is madness, it is flinging away our liberties, not only without a struggle, but without the slightest concern, at the first appearance of the enemy.

Before entering upon this subject, I would premise that the course of the Courier and Enquirer, and the Star, on the one side, and that of the Evening Post, the Times, and their coadjutors, on the other, are equally hostile to the safety of the country. I am for an American party, but not that American party advocated by the Evening Star, which Journal, while announcing its formation upon principles "*distinct from party*," in the same breath gives it an *anti-administration* character, and attempts to wield it against the principles of Mr. Van Buren. Neither on the other hand will the stanch supporters of the Democratic principles which have governed the present Administration, and who still mean to support Mr. Van Buren, as the representative of their sentiments, be turned from their course of determined and persevering resistance to *foreign interference*, by the unfounded charge that the American party which they support is exclusively, or even at all, of Whig origin. The writer of this will give his own political views, solely for the purpose of silencing the unfounded charges made against a cause in its commencement, which he feels assured is to connect in its support all true Patriots, whatever may be their party predilections. His own political principles have been the same for more than 20 years, and they are those now so ably represented by Mr. Van Buren and the present Administration. They are the Democratic principles of the Jefferson school, as they stand opposed to *Aristocracy* in all its shapes, to ruinous *Monopolies*, to a union of *Church and State*, and to all kindred evils; they are, in short, the principles which are distinctive of American institutions, principles opposed most thoroughly to absolute or priestly power. And the stand he now takes, results from the firm conviction, that these very principles are all endangered by *the present state of our naturalization laws*, which have assumed *a new aspect in consequence of political movements in Europe*, and the undue influence which naturalized citizens in their foreign capacity have been made to exert in the political contests of the country. The *political state of Europe; the particular movements which have caused this stand to be taken; the dangers of the State in consequence of these foreign movements;* and *the Remedy proposed*, will be briefly discussed in future numbers; and it is believed that the necessity of a true American party, uniting Americans of every party, will be found necessary to ward off a blow aimed at the very foundations of our government; and before either party commits itself on a question, which in spite of all they can do will agitate this whole land, let them examine carefully its merits. Let those who have been so hasty to condemn before the cause is tried, suspend their judgment awhile, nor rashly take a course which will oblige them either to incur the humiliation of defeat, or the almost equally unpleasant task of retraction.

No. II.

The difference of condition of the alien in Europe and in America.—Brief glance at the great steps of political advancement in Europe.—*Action* of American principles on Europe.—*Reaction*, perfectly natural.—Proofs of its actual existence.—The Combination in Europe to react on America.—The St. Leopold Foundation.

OUR country, in the position it has given to foreigners who have made it their home, has pursued a course in relation to them, totally different from that of any other country in the world. This course, while it is liberal without example, subjects our institutions to peculiar dangers. In all other countries the foreigner, to whatever privileges he may be entitled by becoming a subject, can never be placed in a situation to be politically dangerous, for he has no share in the government of the country; even in England, he has no political influence, for even *after naturalization* an alien cannot become a member of the House of Commons, or of the Privy Council, or hold offices or grants under the Crown.

In the other countries of Europe, the right of naturalization in each particular case, belongs to the Executive branch of government. It is so in France, in Bavaria, and all the German States. In France, indeed, a residence of 10 years gives to the alien all the rights of a citizen, even that of becoming a member of the Chamber of Deputies, but the limited *suffrage* in that country operates as a check on any abuse of this privilege.

This country on the contrary opens to the foreigner, without other check than an oath, that he has resided five years in the country, a direct influence on its political affairs.

This country, therefore, stands alone, without guide from the example of any other; and I am to show in the sequel some of the peculiar dangers to which our situation in this respect exposes us. But the better to comprehend these dangers, let me briefly trace the prominent steps in European politics which connect the past with the present.

Europe has been generally at rest from war for some 20 years past. The activity of mind which had so long been engaged in war, in military schemes of offence and defence in the field, was, at the general pacification of the world, to be transferred to the Cabinet, and turned to the cultivation of the arts of peace. It was at this period of a General Peace, that a Holy Alliance of the Monarchs of Europe was formed. The Sovereigns professed to be guided by the maxims of religion, and with holy motives seemed solicitous only for the peace of the world. But they have long since betrayed that their plans of tranquillity were to be intimately connected with the preservation of their own arbitrary power, and the destruction of popular liberty every where. Whatever militated against this power, or favoured this liberty, was to be crushed. To this single end has been directed all the diplomatic talent of Europe for years. The "General Peace" was, and still is, the ever ready plea in excuse for every new act of oppression at home, or of interference abroad. The mental elements, however, set in motion remotely by the *Protestant Reformation*, but more strongly agitated by *the American Revolution*, are yet working among the people of these governments to give the Tyrants of the earth uneasiness. Conspiracies and Revolutions in the more absolute governments, (as in Austria, Russia, and the smaller States, Italy, Holland, Belgium, &c.,) and the alternate changes from more to less arbitrary components in the Cabinets of the more popular governments, (as in England, France, and Switzerland,) indicate to us at various times the vicissitudes of the great contest, and the sharpness of the struggle. This being the political condition of Europe, easily shown to have grown out of the great divisions of *free* and *despotic* principles, made at the Reformation, is it at all likely that the happy fruits of this Reformation, more completely developed in this land of liberty, and exhibited perpetually to the gaze of all the world, can have had no influence upon the despotisms of Europe? Can the example of Democratic liberty which this country shows, produce no uneasiness to monarchs? Does not every day bring fresh intelligence of the influence of American Democracy *directly* in England, France, Spain, Portugal, and Belgium, and *indirectly* in all the other European countries? And is there no danger of a *re-action* from Europe? Have we no interest in these changing aspects of European politics? The writer believes, that since the time of the American Revolution, which gave the principles of Democratic liberty a home, those principles have never been in greater jeopardy than at the present moment. To his reasons for thus believing, he invites the unimpassioned investigation of every American citizen. If there is danger, let it arouse to defence. If it is a false alarm, let such explanations be given of most suspicious appearances as shall safely allay it. It is no *party* question, and the attempt to make it one, should be at once suspected. It concerns all of every party.

There is danger of re-action from Europe; and it is the part of common prudence to look for it, and to provide against it. The great political truth has recently been promulged at the capital of one of the principal courts of Europe, at Vienna, and by one of the profoundest scholars of Germany, (Frederick Schlegel, a devoted Roman Catholic, and one of the Austrian Cabinet,) the great truth, clearly and unanswerably proved, that the *political revolutions to which European governments have been so long subjected, from the popular desires for liberty, are the natural effects of the Protestant Reformation.* That *Protestantism* favours *Republicanism,* while *Popery* as naturally supports *Monarchical* power. In these lectures, delivered by Schlegel for the purpose of strengthening the cause of absolute power, at the time that he was Counsellor of Legation in the Austrian Cabinet, and the confidential friend of Prince Metternich, there is a *most important* allusion to this country; and as it demonstrates one of the principal connecting points between European and American politics, and is the key to many of the mysterious doings that are in operation against American institutions under our own eyes, let Americans treasure it well in their memories. This is the passage:—"THE GREAT NURSERY *of these destructive principles,* (the principles of Democracy,) *the* GREAT REVOLUTIONARY SCHOOL *for* FRANCE *and* THE REST OF EUROPE, *is* NORTH AMERICA!" Yes, (I address Democratic Americans,) the influence of this Republican government, of your democratic system, is vitally felt by Austria. She confesses it. It is proscribed by the Austrian Cabinet. This country is designated directly to all her people, and to her allied despots, as the great *plague spot* of the world, the poisoned fountain whence flow all the deadly evils which threaten their own existence. Is there nothing intended by this language of Austria? The words of Despots are few, but they are full of meaning. If action, indeed, did not follow their speeches, they might be safely indulged in their harmless proscriptions. But this is not the case.—Austria has followed out her words into actions. Is it wonderful after such an avowal in regard to America, that she should do something to rid herself and the world of such a tremendous evil? Does not her own existence in truth depend upon destroying our example? Would it not be worth all the treasures of wealth that she could collect, if they could but purchase this great good? But how shall she attack us? She cannot send her armies, they would be useless. She has told us by the mouth of her Counsellor of Legation, that Popery, while it is the natural antagonist to Protestantism, is opposed in its whole character to Republican liberty, and is the promoter and supporter of arbitrary power. How fitted then is Popery for her purpose! This she can send without alarming our fears, or, at least, only the fears of those "*miserable,*" "*intolerant fanatics,*" and "*pious bigots,*" who affect to see danger to the liberties of the country in the mere introduction of a *religious system* opposed to their own, and whose cry of danger, be it ever so loud, will only be regarded as the result of "*sectarian fear,*" and the plot ridiculed as a *quixotic dream.*" But is there any thing so irrational in such a scheme? Is it not the most natural and obvious act for Austria to do, with her views of the influence of Popery upon the form of government, its influence to pull down Republicanism, and build up monarchy; I say, is it not her most obvious act *to send Popery to this country if it is not here, or give it a fresh and vigorous impulse if it is already here?* At any rate *she is doing it.* She has set herself to work with all her activity to disseminate throughout the country the *Popish religion.* Immediately after the delivery of Schlegel's lectures, which was in the year 1828, a great society was formed in the Austrian capital, in Vienna, in 1829. The late Emperor, and Prince Metternich, and the Crown Prince, (now Emperor,) and all the civil and ecclesiastical officers of the empire, with the princes of Savoy and Piedmont, uniting in it, and calling it after the name of a canonized King, *St. Leopold.* This society is formed for a great and express purpose. It has all the officers of government interested in it, from the Emperor down to the humblest in the Empire; and what is this purpose? Why, that "*of promoting the greater activity of Catholic missions in America;*" these are the words of their own reports. Yes; these Foreign despots are suddenly stirred up to combine and promote the greater activity of Popery in this country; and this, too, just after they had been convinced of the truth, or, more properly speaking, had their memories quickened with it, that *Popery is utterly opposed to Republican liberty*. These are the facts in the case. Americans, explain them in your own way. If any choose to stretch their charity so far as to believe that these crowned gentlemen have combined in this Society solely for *religious* purposes; that they have organized a Society to collect moneys to be spent in this country, and have sent Jesuits as their almoners, and ship-loads of Roman Catholic emigrants, and for the sole purpose of converting us to the *religion* of Popery, and without any *political* design, credat Judæus Apella, non ego.

No. III.

The extent of the St. Leopold Foundation.—Its agents in this country.—Jesuits.—Their Character.—Their tricks already visible, in the riotous *Ultraism* of the day.

I HAVE shown that a Society, (the "*St. Leopold Foundation*") is organized in a Foreign Absolute government, having its central direction in the capital of that government at Vienna, under the patronage of the Emperor of Austria, and the other Despotic Rulers,—a Society for the purpose of spreading Popery in this country. Of this fact there is no doubt. This "*St. Leopold Foundation*" has its ramifications through the whole of the Austrian empire. It is not a small private association, but *a great and extensive combination*. It embraces in its extent, as shown by their own documents, not merely the wide Austrian Empire, Hungary, and Italy, but it includes Piedmont, Savoy, and Catholic France; it embodies the civil and ecclesiastical authorities of all these countries. And is such an extensive combination in foreign countries for the avowed purpose of operating in this country, (no matter for what purpose,) so trivial an affair, that we may safely dismiss it with a sneer? Have these foreign Rulers so much sympathy with our system of government, that we may trust them safely to meddle with it, in *any way?* Are they so impotent in combination as to excite in us no alarm? May they send money, and agents, and a system of government wholly at variance with our own, and spread it through all our borders with impunity from our search, because it is nick-named *Religion?* There was a time when American sensibilities were quick on the subject of *foreign interference*. What has recently deadened them?

Let us examine the operations of this Austrian Society, for it is hard at work all around us; yes, here in this country, from one end to the other, at our very doors, in this city. From a machinery of such a character and power, we shall doubtless be able to see already some effect. With its head-quarters at Vienna, under the immediate direction and inspection of Metternich, the well-known *great managing general of the diplomacy* of Europe, it makes itself already felt through the republic. Its emissaries are here. And who are these emissaries? They are JESUITS. This society of men, after exerting their tyranny for upwards of 200 years, at length became so formidable to the world, threatening the entire subversion of all social order, that even the Pope, whose *devoted subjects* they are, and must be, by the vow of their society, was compelled to dissolve them. They had not been suppressed, however, for 50 years, before the waning influence of Popery and Despotism required their useful labours, to resist the spreading light of Democratic liberty, and the Pope, (Pius VII,) simultaneously with the formation of the Holy Alliance, revived the order of the Jesuits in all their power. From their vow of "*unqualified submission to the Sovereign Pontiff*," they have been appropriately called the *Pope's body guard*. It should be known, that *Austrian influence elected the present Pope;* his body guard are therefore at the service of Austria, and these are the soldiers that the Leopold Society has sent to this country, and they are agents of this society, to execute its designs, whatever these designs may be. And do Americans need to be told what *Jesuits* are? If any are ignorant, let them inform themselves of their history without delay; no time is to be lost: their workings are before you in every day's events: they are a *secret* society, a sort of Masonic order, with superadded features of most revolting odiousness, and a thousand times more dangerous. They are not confined to one class in society; they are not merely priests, or priests of one religious creed, they are merchants, and lawyers, and editors, and men of any profession, and no profession, having no outward badge, (in this country,) by which to be recognised; they are about in all your society. They can assume any character, that of angels of light, or ministers of darkness, to accomplish their one great end, the *service* upon which they are sent, whatever that service may be. "They are all educated men, prepared, and sworn to *start at any moment, in any direction,* and for any service, commanded by the general of their order, bound to no family, community, or country, by the ordinary ties which bind men; and *sold for life* to the cause of the Roman Pontiff."

These are the men at this moment ordered to America. And can they do nothing, Americans, to derange the free workings of your democratic institutions? Can they not, and do they not fan the slightest embers of discontent into a flame, those thousand little differences which must perpetually occur in any society, into riot, *and quell its excess among their own people as it suits their policy and the establishment of their own control?* Yes, they can be the aggressors, and contrive to be the aggrieved. They can do the mischief, and manage to be publicly lauded for their praiseworthy forbearance and their suffering patience. They can persecute, and turn away the popular indignation, ever roused by the cry of persecution from themselves, and make it fall upon their victim. They can *control the press* in a thousand secret ways. They can write under the signature of "Whig," to-day, and if it suits their turn, "Tory," to-morrow. They can be Democrat to-day, and Aristocrat to-morrow. They can out-American Americans in admiration of American institutions to-day, and "condemn them as unfit for any people" to-morrow. These are the men that Austria has sent here, that she supplies with money, with whom she keeps up an active correspondence, and whose officers (the Bishops) are passing back and forth between Europe and America, doubtless to impart that information *orally* which would not be so safe committed to writing.

Is there no danger to the Democracy of the country from such formidable foes arrayed against it? Is Metternich its friend? Is the *Pope* its friend? Are his official documents, now daily put forth, *Democratic* in their character?

O there is no danger to the Democracy; for those most devoted to the Pope, the Roman Catholics, especially the Irish Catholics, are all on the side of Democracy. Yes; to be sure they are on the side of Democracy. They are just where I should look for them. Judas Iscariot joined with the true disciples. Jesuits are not fools. They would not startle our slumbering fears, by bolting out their monarchical designs directly in our teeth, and by joining the opposing ranks, *except so far as to cover their designs.* This is a Democratic country, and the Democratic party is and ever must be the strongest party, unless ruined by traitors and Jesuits in the camp. Yes; it is in the ranks of Democracy I should expect to find them, and for no good purpose be assured. Every measure of Democratic policy in the least exciting will be pushed to *ultraism,* so soon as it is introduced for discussion. Let every real Democrat guard against this common Jesuitical artifice of tyrants, an artifice which there is much evidence to believe is practising against them at this moment, an artifice *which if not heeded will surely be the ruin of Democracy:* it is founded on the well-known principle that "*extremes meet.*" The writer has seen it pass under his own eyes in Europe, in more than one instance. When in despotic governments popular discontent, arising from the intolerable oppressions of the tyrants of the people, has manifested itself by popular outbreakings, to such a degree as to endanger the throne, and the people seemed prepared to shove their masters from their horses, and are likely to mount, and seize the reins themselves; then, the popular movement, unmanageable any longer by resistance, is pushed to the extreme. The passions of the ignorant and vicious are excited to outrage by pretended friends of the people. Anarchy ensues; and then the mass of the people, who are always lovers of order and quiet, unite at once in support of the strong arm of force for protection; and despotism, perhaps, in another, but *preconcerted* shape, resumes its iron reign. Italy and Germany are furnishing examples every day. If an illustration is wanted on a larger scale, look at France in her late Republican revolution, and in her present relapse into despotism.

He who would prevent you from mounting his horse, has two ways of thwarting your designs. If he finds your efforts to rise too strong for his resistance, he has but to add a little more impulse to them, and he shoves you over on the other side. In either case you are on the ground.

No. IV.

The Despotism inherent in Jesuitism exposed.—The folly of the outcry of Persecution, Intolerance, &c., raised against this discussion.—The character of the foreign materials, with which Jesuits can work injury to the Republic.

THAT Jesuits are at work upon the passions of the American community, managing in various ways to gain control, must be evident to all. They who have learned from history the general mode of proceeding of this crafty set of men, could easily infer that they were here, even were it not otherwise confirmed by unquestionable evidence in their correspondence with their foreign masters in Austria. There are some, perhaps, who are under the impression that the order of Jesuits is a purely religious Society for the dissemination of the Roman Catholic religion; and therefore comes within the protection of our laws, and must be tolerated. There cannot be a greater mistake. It was from the beginning a *political* organization, an absolute Monarchy masked by religion. It has been aptly styled "*tyranny by religion.*" If any doubt on this subject is entertained, let the following from their own documents dispel it. In an authorized work of theirs, they say:

"The members of the Society of Jesuits are dispersed through all nations of the world, and *divided only by distance of place*, NOT IN SENTIMENT; by difference in language, not in affection; by variety of colour, not in manner. In this fraternity, the Latin, Greek, Portuguese, Brazilian, Irish, Sumatran, Spanish, French, English, and Belgic Jesuits, ALL THINK, FEEL, SPEAK, AND ACT ALIKE; for among them there is neither debate nor contention. [Imago. Soc. Jes. Proleg. p. 33.] The SAME DESIGN, and COURSE OF ACTION, and *one vow only, like the conjugal bond, unite the order together*." [Ibid. lib. 5. p. 622.]

We are then clearly authorized by themselves, to impute to the Jesuits, in this country, the same *sentiments* and *design*, and *cause of action* as are avowed by their brethren abroad. Let us see what these are; and I ask American Democrats especially to look at this. There was an address presented to the King of Spain, not in the dark ages, not by a former Society of Jesuits, but to Ferdinand VII., whose character we all know, and who died but a short time ago; an address by one of this order of Jesuits, since their revival in 1814. Vallestigny, a deputy of Alva, a Jesuit, in this address to his Majesty, says, "*The mass of the human family are born, not to govern, but to be governed.* This sublime employment of governing *has been confided* by Providence *to the privileged class*, whom he has placed upon an eminence *to which the multitude cannot rise* without being lost in the labyrinth and snares which are therein found." [Archbishop de Pradt.] Is this Democracy? Look at it seriously. The Jesuits in this country must by their own confession have the same sentiments; and yet, with the cunning and duplicity of their craft, they have allied themselves to our party. Why is this? It is easily explained. Every body knows how readily, in moments of strong party feeling, we imbibe the opinions, even without examination, of those who sympathize with us. Do not Jesuits know this, and are they not taking advantage of our very love to our own institutions, to quiet our fears and to obtain our protection and aid while they organize themselves, and extend their influence more thoroughly in the country, preparatory to compassing their future designs? And will these designs be in favour of Democracy? Let them speak for themselves in the sentiments I have quoted. It becomes important to inquire, then, what are the *principal materials* in our society with which Jesuits can accomplish the political designs of the Foreign Despots embodied in the Leopold Foundation. And here let me make the passing remark, that there has been a great deal of mawkish sensitiveness on the subject of introducing any thing concerning religion into political discussions. This sensitiveness, as it is not merely foolish, arising from ignorance of the true line which separates political and theological matters, but also exposes the political interests of the country to manifest danger, I am glad to see is giving way to a proper feeling on the subject. Church and State must be for ever separated, but it is the height of folly to suppose, that in political discussions, *Religion* especially, the *political* character *of any and every religious creed* may not be publicly discussed. The absurdity of such a position is too manifest to dwell a moment upon it. And in considering the materials in our society adapted to the purposes of hostile attack upon our Institutions, we must of necessity notice the Roman Catholic religion. *It is this form of religion* that is most implicated in the conspiracy against our liberties. It is in this sect that the Jesuits are organized. It is this sect that is proclaimed by one of its own most brilliant and profound literary men to be *hostile in its very nature to republican liberty;* and it is the active extension of this sect that Austria is endeavouring to promote throughout this Republic. And Americans will not be cowed into silence by the cries of *persecution, intolerance, bigotry, fanaticism,* and such puerile catchwords, perpetually uttered against those who speak or write ever so calmly against the dangers of Popery. I can say, once for all, that no such outcry weighs a feather with me, nor does it weigh a feather with the mass of the American people. They have good sense enough to discriminate, especially in a subject of such vital importance to their safety, between *words* and *things.* I am not tenacious of *words,* except for convenience sake, the better to be understood, but if detestation of Jesuitism and tyranny, whether in a civil or ecclesiastical shape, is in future to be called *intolerance,* be it so; only let it be generally understood, and I will then glory in *intolerance.* When that which is now esteemed *virtue,* is to be known by general consent only by the name *vice,* why I will not be singular, but glory in *vice,* since the word is used to embody the *essential qualities of virtue.* I will just add, that those who are so fond of employing these epithets, forget that by so constantly, loosely, and indiscriminately using them, they cease to convey any meaning, or to excite any emotions but those of disgust towards those who use them.

To return to the subject; it is in the Roman Catholic ranks that we are principally to look for the materials to be employed by the Jesuits, and in what condition do we find this sect at present in our country? We find it spreading itself into every nook and corner of the land; churches, chapels, colleges, nunneries and convents, are springing up as if by magic every where; an activity hitherto unknown among the Roman Catholics pervades all their ranks, and yet whence the means for all these efforts? Except here and there funds or favours collected from an inconsistent *Protestant,* (*so called* probably because born in a Protestant country, who is flattered or wheedled by some Jesuit artifice to give his aid to their cause,) the greatest part of the pecuniary means for all these works are from abroad. They are the contributions of his Majesty the Emperor of Austria, of Prince Metternich, of the late Charles X., and the other Despots combined in the Leopold Society. And who are the members of the Roman Catholic communion? What proportion are natives of this land, nurtured under our own institutions, and well versed in the nature of American liberty? Is it not notorious that the greater part are *Foreigners* from the various Catholic countries of Europe. Emigration has of late years been specially promoted among this class of Foreigners, and they have been in the proportion of three to one of all other emigrants arriving on our shores; they are from Ireland, Germany, Poland, and Belgium. From about the period of the formation of the Leopold Society, Catholic emigration increased in an amazing degree.* Colonies of Emigrants, selected, perhaps, with a view to occupy particular places, (for, be it remembered, every portion of this country is as perfectly known at Vienna and Rome as in any part of our own country,) have been constantly arriving. The principal emigrants are from Ireland and Germany. We have lately been told by the captain of a lately arrived *Austrian vessel*, which, by the by, brought 70 emigrants from *Antwerp!* that a desire is suddenly manifested among the poorer class of the Belgian population, to emigrate to America. They are mostly, if not all, Roman Catholics, be it remarked, for Belgium is a Catholic country, and *Austrian vessels are bringing them here.* Whatever *the cause* of all this movement abroad to send to this country their poorer classes, the fact is certain, the class of emigrants is known, and the instrument, Austria, is seen in it —the same power that directs the Leopold Foundation.

No. V.

The great mass of Emigrants necessarily under the control of Catholic priests.—Mr. Jefferson's warning against the dangers of Foreign Emigration.—The evils he predicted now occurring.—O'Connell interfering in the *American* Slavery question.

I HAVE shown what are the *Foreign materials* imported into the country, with which the Jesuits can work to accomplish their designs. Let us examine this point a little more minutely. These materials are the *varieties of Foreigners* of the same Creed, the Roman Catholic, over all of whom the Bishops or Vicars General hold, as a matter of course, ecclesiastical rule; and we well know what is the nature of Roman Catholic ecclesiastical rule,—it is the double refined spirit of despotism, which, after arrogating to itself the prerogatives of Deity, and so claiming to bind or loose the *soul* eternally, makes it, in the comparison, but a mere trifle to exercise absolute sway in all that relates to the body. The notorious ignorance in which the great mass of these emigrants have been all their lives sunk, until their minds are dead, makes them but senseless machines; they obey orders mechanically, for it is the habit of their education, in the despotic countries of their birth. And can it be for a moment supposed by any one that by the act of coming to this country, and being naturalized, their darkened intellects can suddenly be illuminated to discern the nice boundary where their *ecclesiastical obedience* to their priests *ends*, and their *civil independence* of them *begins?* The very supposition is absurd. They obey their priests as demigods, from the habit of their whole lives; they have been taught from infancy that their priests are infallible in the greatest matters, and can they, by mere importation to this country, be suddenly imbued with the knowledge that in civil matters their priests may err, and that they are not in these also their infallible guides? Who will teach them this? Will their priests? Let common sense answer this question. Must not the priests, as a matter almost of *certainty*, control the opinions of their ignorant flock in civil as well as religious matters? and do they not do it?

Mr. Jefferson, with that deep sagacity and foresight which distinguished him as a politician, foresaw, predicted, and issued his warning, on the great danger to

* A check at this moment, *apparently unaccountable*, has suddenly occurred in Emigration. This I think is capable of an easy solution. It may be that foreign fears were excited lest Americans might become alarmed at so great an increase of foreigners. There may be other causes, but I must suspect all the doings of Jesuits. N. B. Since the publication of this number, *emigration* has taken a fresh start. From 1st July to 1st of August, 1835, a single month, there arrived in the port of New-York alone, SIX THOUSAND EIGHT HUNDRED AND TWENTY-TWO Emigrants, which is at the annual rate of upwards of 80,000; and this, be it remembered, is only at *one* point in the country!

the country of this introduction of foreigners. He doubted its policy, even when the advantages seemed to be greatest. He says, "The present desire of America, (in 1781,) is to produce rapid population by as great *importations of foreigners* as possible. *But is this founded in policy?*" * * * "Are there no *inconveniences* to be thrown into the scale against the advantage expected from a multiplication of numbers by the importation of foreigners? It is for the happiness of those united in society to harmonize as much as possible in matters which they must of necessity transact together.

"Civil government being the sole object of forming societies, its administration must be conducted by common consent. Every species of government has its specific principles. Ours, perhaps, are more peculiar than those of any other in the universe. It is a composition of the freest principles of the English constitution, with others derived from natural right, and natural reason. To these nothing can be more opposed than the maxims of absolute monarchies. Yet, from such, we are to expect the greatest number of emigrants. *They will bring with them the principles of the governments they leave, imbibed in their early youth; or, if able to throw them off, it will be in exchange for an unbounded licentiousness*, passing, as is usual, from one extreme to another. It would be a miracle were they to stop precisely at the point of temperate liberty. These principles, with their language, they will transmit to their children. *In proportion to their numbers, they will share with us the legislation. They will infuse into it their spirit, warp and bias its directions, and render it a heterogeneous, incoherent, distracted mass.*"

"I may appeal to experience, for a verification of these conjectures. But if they be not *certain in event*, are they not *possible, are they not probable?* Is it not safer to wait with patience—for the attainment of any degree of population desired or expected? May not our government be more homogeneous, more peaceable, more durable?" He asks what would be the condition of France if 20 millions of Americans were suddenly imported into that kingdom? and adds—"If it would be *more turbulent*, less happy, less strong, we may believe that the addition of *half a million of foreigners* would produce a *similar effect here.*"

So long an extract in point from Mr. Jefferson, needs no apology. The fears of that great statesman were prophetic, and we of these days are experiencing the fruits partly of our own folly, partly of Foreign Conspiracy taking advantage of this folly.

What was dimly seen by the prophetic eye of Jefferson, is actually passing under our own eyes. Already have foreigners increased in the country to such a degree, that they justly give us alarm. They feel themselves so strong, as to organize themselves even as *foreigners* into *foreign bands*, and this for the purpose of influencing our elections. But a bolder step has been hazarded within a few weeks. A *portion of foreigners* have had the audacity to attempt the formation of themselves into a separate MILITARY CORPS, and at this moment to take the name of a foreigner who, whatever qualities he may possess to make him admired in his own country and among his own religious sect, has very few points, if any, in common with Americans, and has lately denounced a vengeance on this whole nation, to which Americans when they are inclined to cry peace to themselves, would do well to turn their thoughts, especially when they connect the facts, that he who has denounced the South especially, and thrown a firebrand into the *Slavery* question, is the *great Agitator*, so called, that he is an Irishman and a Roman Catholic, that the great mass of the foreigners in this country of the same sect are from Ireland. That they are men who having *professed* to become Americans, by accepting our terms of naturalization, do yet, in direct contradiction to their professions, clan together as a separate interest, and retain their foreign appellation; that it is with such a separate foreign interest, organizing in the midst of us, that Jesuits in the pay of foreign powers are tampering; that it is this foreign corps of religionists that Americans of both parties have been for years in the habit of basely and traitorously encouraging to erect into an umpire of our political divisions, thus virtually surrendering the government into the hands of Despotic powers. In view of these facts, which every day's experience proves to be facts, is it not time, high time, that a true American spirit were roused to resist this alarming inroad of foreign influence upon our institutions, to avert dangers to which we have hitherto shut our eyes, and which if not remedied, and that immediately, will inevitably change the whole character of our government. I repeat what I first said, this is no party question, it concerns native Americans of all parties.

No. VI.

Recapitulation of Facts.—The necessity and propriety of discussing the political nature of the Roman Catholic System.

I HAVE set forth in a very brief and imperfect manner the evil, the great and increasing evil, that threatens our free institutions from *foreign interference*. Have I not shown that there is real cause for alarm? Let me recapitulate the facts in the case, and see if any one of them can be denied; and if not, I submit it to the calm decision of every American, whether he can still sleep in fancied security, while incendiaries are at work; and whether he is ready quietly to surrender his liberty, civil and religious, into the hands of foreign powers.

1. It is a fact, that in this age the subject of civil and religious liberty agitates in the most intense manner the various European governments.

2. It is a fact, that the influence of American free institutions in subverting European despotic institutions is greater now than it has ever been, from the fact of the greater maturity, and long-tried character, of the American form of government.

3. It is a fact, that Popery is opposed in its very nature to Democratic Republicanism; and it is, therefore, as a political system, as well as religious, opposed to civil and religious liberty, and consequently to our form of government.

4. It is a fact, that this truth, respecting the intrinsic character of Popery, has lately been clearly and demonstratively proved in public lectures, by one of the Austrian Cabinet, a devoted Roman Catholic, and with the evident design (as subsequent events show) of exciting the Austrian government to a great enterprise in support of absolute power.

5. It is a fact, that this Member of the Austrian Cabinet, in his lectures, designated and proscribed this country by name, as the "*great nursery of destructive principles; as the Revolutionary school for France and the rest of Europe,*" whose contagious example of Democratic liberty had given, and would still give, trouble to the rest of the world, unless the evil were abated.

6. It is a fact, that very shortly after the delivery of these lectures, a Society was organized in the Austrian capital, called the St. Leopold Foundation, for the purpose "of promoting the greater activity of Catholic Missions in America."

7. It is a fact, that this Society is under the patronage of the Emperor of Austria,—has its central direction at Vienna,—is under the supervision of Prince Metternich,—that it is an extensive combination, embodying the civil, as well as ecclesiastical *officers*, not only of the *whole Austrian Empire*, but of the neighbouring Despotic States,—that it is actively at work, collecting moneys, and sending agents to this country, to carry into effect its designs.

8. It is a fact, that the agents of these foreign despots, are, for the most part, *Jesuits*.

9. It is a fact, that the effects of this society are already apparent in the otherwise unaccountable increase of Roman Catholic cathedrals, churches, colleges, convents, nunneries, &c., in every part of the country; in the sudden increase of Catholic emigration; in the increased clanishness of the Roman Catholics, and the boldness with which their leaders are experimenting on the character of the American people.

10. It is a fact, that an unaccountable disposition to riotous conduct has manifested itself within a few years, when exciting topics are publicly discussed, wholly at variance with the former peaceful, deliberative character of our people.

11. It is a fact, that a species of police, unknown to our laws, has repeatedly been put in requisition to keep the peace among a certain class of foreigners, who are Roman Catholics, viz., Priest-police.

12. It is a fact, that Roman Catholic Priests have interfered to influence our elections.

13. It is a fact, that politicians on both sides have propitiated these priests, to obtain the votes of their people.

14. It is a fact, that numerous Societies of Roman Catholics, particularly among the Irish foreigners, are organized in various parts of the country, under various names, and ostensibly for certain benevolent objects; that these societies are united together by correspondence, all which may be innocent and praiseworthy, but, viewed in connexion with the recent aspect of affairs, are at least suspicious.*

15. It is a fact, that an attempt has been made to organize a military corps of Irishmen in New-York, to be called the O'Connel Guards; thus commencing a military organization of foreigners.

16. It is a fact, that the greater part of the foreigners in our population is composed of Roman Catholics.

Facts like these I have enumerated might be multiplied, but these are the most important, and quite sufficient to make every American settle the question with himself, whether there is, or is not, danger to the country from the present state of our Naturalization Laws. I have stated what I believe to be facts. If they are *not* facts, they will easily be disproved, and I most sincerely hope they will be disproved. If they are facts, and my inferences from them are wrong, I can be shown where I have erred, and an inference more rational, and more probable, involving less, or perhaps no, danger to the country, can be deduced from them, which deduction, when I see it, I will most cheerfully accept, as a full explanation of these most suspicious doings of Foreign Powers.

I have spoken in these numbers freely of a particular religious sect, the Roman Catholics, because from the nature of the case it was unavoidable; because the foreign political conspiracy is identified with that creed. With the *religious tenets* properly so called, of the Roman Catholic, I have not meddled. If foreign powers, hostile to the principles of this government, have combined to spread any religious creed, no matter of what denomination, that creed does by that very act become a subject of political interest to all citizens, and must and will be thoroughly scrutinized. We are compelled to examine it. We have no choice about it. If instead of combining to spread with the greatest activity the Catholic Religion throughout our country, the Monarchs of Europe had united to spread Presbyterianism, or Methodism, I presume, there are few who would not see at once the propriety and the necessity of looking most narrowly at the political bearings of the peculiar principles of these Sects, or of any other Protestant Sects; and members of any Protestant Sects too, would be the last to complain of the examination. I know not why the Roman Catholics in this land of scrutiny are to plead exclusive exemption from the same trial.

No. VII.

The various plans for a change in the Naturalization Laws examined.—The ridiculous claim set up for the foreigner to *superior* rights, exposed.—American birthright vindicated.

I HAD completed that part of my original plan, in which I exposed the dangers to our institutions from *a foreign reaction*, naturally to be expected from the present political condition of Europe, as well as of our own country. I have shown undeniably, (for none of my *facts* have been denied, and, let it be noticed, they are of

* Appendix, (1.)

the most serious character,) that the danger from an insidious foreign interference, already in active operation under cover of the professedly *religious* society of combined despots, called the St. Leopold Foundation, was imminent, and that this danger was enhanced by the great increase of the most degraded class of foreign emigrants; by their natural unfitness for citizenship, more particularly from their want of mental independence. To this danger, the facility afforded by our Naturalization Laws for bestowing on them the rights of citizenship, gives a character of tenfold seriousness. That a change of some kind in the Naturalization Laws is required, seems to be conceded on all sides, but the nature and extent of this change are strangely opposite in character. While some, and doubtless the greater part of the American population, would have them changed with the view of *discouraging* immigration, and of guarding our institutions from foreign interference, at the point where they are not only assailable, but where they are at this moment actually assailed and greatly endangered; others would have them changed so as to throw down all the barriers which protect us as an independent nation, and extend the right of suffrage, strange as it may seem, with such an unheard of universality of application, as no advocate of the proper and just principles of universal suffrage ever before ventured to dream of; to the extent, in fact, virtually of giving the administration of our government to any and all nations of the world, no matter how barbarous, who choose to take the trouble to exercise it. Instead of guarding with greater vigilance and care our institutions, when attacked, by new defences, these patriots would not only make no resistance, but would actually invite the enemy, by demolishing the fortresses already existing, and yield up the country into his uncontrolled possession. Lest I should be accused of exaggeration, I quote the following from the Evening Post:

"We are not opposed to a change in the Naturalization Laws; but are opposed to any change that would lengthen the probation. In our view of the subject, no good reason can be urged against foreigners being admitted to citizenship *the moment they set foot in the country*, provided they make suitable declaration of their intention of residence. We would make the necessity of such a declaration the only distinction between an emigrant from a foreign country and one from another state of our own country. In both cases the right of suffrage could be exercised only after the term of residence prescribed for all citizens, viz: twelve months in the state, and six months in the particular township or ward."

That those Foreign Jesuits in the country, the travelling and corresponding and editorial agents in the pay and service of the St. Leopold Society, should suggest and advocate such a doctrine as this, so favourable to the accomplishment of their schemes, would not be in the least surprising, for it is completely in character; but I confess, it is truly astonishing that any real true hearted American, such as I believe the editor of the Post to be, should be so absorbed, in I know not what sort of notions of universal philanthropy, as to forget entirely the claims of his own country, in an exclusive fondness for foreigners, and should put forward at this moment so revolting a proposition. I can scarcely believe him serious; yet, if he is, he certainly depends on other means for enforcing a conviction of its soundness or the propriety of its adoption, than either an appeal to American love of country, to American intelligence, or to reason and common sense. If I understand him, he would put the Foreigner, the moment of his landing, on the same footing with native American citizens, no matter from what country he may come, no matter what his early habits, his character or condition, whether Hottentot or Turk, or Russian serf, or New-Zealand cannibal; the moment he sets foot on our shores, and simply signifies a wish to become a citizen, he is to be a citizen. He would in fact give foreigners of all kinds, not merely the protection, and instruction, and other advantages of citizenship, but the privilege also of electing our rulers; yes, and of being themselves preferred and elected over native Americans. He seems to consider that being born in America is not only no privilege, but an actual demerit, (compared with being born in Ireland, for example,) an unfortunate accident to be ashamed of, rather than boasted of. This I am compelled to believe to be his meaning, for the whole tendency of his journal when treating of this topic, and much am I surprised and chagrined at the fact, is to throw ridicule* and contempt upon sacred love of country, the country of one's birth, to repudiate those universally hallowed affections for native land that cling around the heart of man, whatever his condition, and wherever the place of his birth. I cannot believe that sentiments so revolting, sentiments outraging the warmest feelings of every American bosom, can have been the spontaneous suggestions of his own honest heart. Other journals in the *foreign interest*, and *edited by foreigners*, (and such journals are actually thrust into our hands,) hold the same anti-American tone. Reluctant then as I am to consider this revolting proposal as serious, I must so consider it, for it appears but too evidently supported by the Evening Post whenever foreigners, or the Naturalization Laws are alluded to in that journal. Agreeing as I do in other great political points with the party whose cause the able editor of the Post so creditably advocates, I yet on this separate point can never approve the course pursued of late by more than one journal of the Democratic party. If by their course I am to understand that it is a cardinal party point, then on this, I hesitate not to avow my open persevering hostility. I will not allow for one moment that *American birthright* is to be humbled and annihilated at the feet of a foreign interest; that it is to be trampled on, and mocked by any and all whom foreign despots choose to ship to this country, whether their more knowing stipendiaries, or the ignorant refuse of their poor houses and prisons.—I will never again on any considerations whatever, knowingly assent to confide, to any man of *foreign birth*, (I care not how well fitted for office, or how infallibly honest,) those civil and political trusts to the management of which EVERY AMERICAN BY HIS RIGHT OF BIRTH, I repeat it, EVERY AMERICAN BY HIS RIGHT OF BIRTH, has a previous, a paramount claim; and is it possible that we have men among us who would persuade us that American birthright is nothing? We are told, and told seriously too, that the most abject and degraded slave of foreign superstition, set adrift on our shores, has a merit *superior* to native Americans, because, forsooth, the former has made this *the country of his choice*, while natives, having no choice in the matter, are compelled to be Americans whether they will or not. This is the veritable argument, this is the miserable insulting sophistry cast into the faces of Americans.—In what country do I dwell? Is it indeed a delusion that I have a country? I have resided many years in foreign lands under different forms of government, and often when pity and indignation were roused at the sight of the misery and slavery around me, at the sight of the wretched victims of despotism, I have loved to seek relief in the recollection of my own beloved though distant America, to exult in the happiness of her children, to boast of their political and religious freedom. I rejoiced with feelings of gratitude, of an intensity that none but an American exile can fully appreciate, that Providence had allowed me to call this happy country my own *native* land. And am I now to be told that my birthright is a delusion? Are my countrymen ready to yield theirs to the arrogant demand of those whom they have hitherto supposed the grateful recipients of their hospitality, but who now, strangely and imprudently emboldened, demand the keys of the house and the right of possession? Has it come to this, that an American is compelled to argue such a point with Americans?

* The following from the Evening Post, is an example of the kind of ridicule thrown upon attachment to *native country*:—"An estimable gentleman who formerly resided in this city for many years, but who, like a great many other citizens, had had the misfortune of being first landed in Ireland on his entrance into the world, being once reproached by a rude fellow, during a political contest, with his foreign birth, and the indigence of his circumstances when he first came to this country, good naturedly replied, that there his antagonist was clean at fault, for, said he, 'when I came to America I wore a good coat and a stout pair of leather breeches; whereas, when you came here, you hadn't even a shirt to your back.'—This answer naturally occurs to mind at a time when earnest and daily attempts are making to excite those *who are Americans by the mere accident of birth* against those who are *Americans by choice*, and who left their father-land, braved the dangers of the ocean, and *voluntarily incurred* all the hardships and vicissitudes incident to the emigrant in a strange country *in order to become citizens* under a government of equal laws, and partakers of the blessings of civil and religious freedom."

No. VIII.

Claim of the Foreigner to equal rights with Native Citizens, on the ground of the declared principles of the Government, shown to be groundless.

I EXPOSED, in my last, the ridiculous and presumptuous demand made in behalf of foreigners, to privileges *superior* to native Americans, on the ground of a newly discovered species of merit, to wit: that *birth place being an accident, foreigners who come to this country have made freedom their choice, while native Americans*, by being born in a free country, *had no choice in the matter*, and consequently the former were entitled to privileges *superior to natives*. Truly I have bestowed *too much*, in bestowing *any* notice on such a preposterous argument; were it not for the fact that it appears seriously to be advanced, and seems actually made the foundation of those efforts of foreigners in their various mysterious organizations among us, and which now admit of an easy explanation. They really act on the principle that it is their *right* not merely to receive hospitality at our hands, not merely to be promoted to *equal* rights, but in very deed to seize those *superior privileges* of ruling in this land, because they have made freedom their choice, and come so far to enjoy it. They have doubtless chosen a mode of *making free*, quite original in this country, which only needs the *acquiescence* of Americans, and a little further encouragement, to make it a very grand and successful experiment. I have my doubts, however, whether Americans can be persuaded to allow that any foreigners in this country have better claims to rule than they themselves. At any rate, they are not in the habit generally of acknowledging *superior* claims.

A claim on the part of foreigners to the privileges of our institutions on *equal* terms, is however set up, with more show of plausibility, based as is pretended on the *natural rights* of man, as declared in the *principles of our government*. That such a claim is utterly without foundation, I believe I can satisfactorily show.

The Foreigner, when he arrives on these shores, finds a great insulated community; a large family, separated from all others; independent; each individual of which is bound to the general mass, and the general mass to each individual, in certain mutual and well settled relations. The foreigner presents himself at the door, and claims to be admitted into this community, and to *equal* rights with the rest of the family. On what ground? Why, on that of his *natural rights*, as set forth in our Declaration of Independence. He quotes it, and says, "all men are created equal," "they are endowed with certain unalienable rights, among these are life, liberty, and the pursuit of happiness." 'I am a man, and therefore am entitled, according to your own showing, to equality, and my unalienable rights.' Thus the question seems to him unanswerably settled. Let us examine the matter. The first inquiry respects the meaning of these phrases. If there should be any diversity of opinion as to *what they do mean*, there can at least be no difficulty in ascertaining what they *do* NOT *mean*, which is sufficient to meet the exigencies of this question. It is very clear then that Congress, in the Declaration of Independence, did not mean to allow of *any such construction of that instrument in regard to abstract equality, as should in effect be directly subversive of Independence.* They did not mean to allow of *any construction that must of necessity destroy the common rights of society.* They certainly did not mean by equality *that the minority should be superior or equal to the majority.* They did not mean to sanction such a use of life, liberty, and means of happiness in a single individual, or a *smaller part* of the community, as should destroy or endanger the lives, liberties, or means of happiness of the *whole* community. These points are clear, and they at once settle the question as to the right of foreigners who come to our shores and demand to be admitted into the community on *equal* terms, and plead as their warrant the *declared abstract principles of the government.* If we are indeed an independent nation, we surely have a right to regulate all *admission into* the nation. What is the meaning of *Independence* as applied to a State, or community? It is an existence separate from all others, a disallowance of all foreign interference or control in its affairs. By independence, a State or community wins a right to arrange its own affairs, in its own way ; not only to regulate its internal polity, among its own members, but to determine whether it will or will not admit others from foreign communities into the family ; and if it chooses to admit them, on what terms they may come. Independence includes more ; it includes the right to expel from the State or community, any and all whom it may think uncongenial to its system, or who disturb, or are even likely to disturb its peace. These are the broad and common sense principles included in independence, principles on which not only the general government uniformly acts, but which are recognised in the daily practice of every State, and every municipal government, in every public and private association, nay, even in every family throughout the country. They are principles of liberty to consult each its own happiness independently; liberty to admit or expel from its own body those whom it will, restricted alone in all, by the paramount regulations of the whole body of which each of these communities large or small are but a part. The Naturalization Laws themselves rest on this basis of independence,—on this admitted right of an independent community to expel from, or to admit or refuse admission into its boundaries.

Again, if a foreigner can come into the country, and claim equal privileges by virtue of the right which he says is granted him in the declaration, that "all men are created equal," then there is no hindrance to his claiming a right on the same ground to obtrude himself into any private association or club, yes, even into our family circles! What principle prevents? Such a construction then, not only annihilates independence, but is subversive of the commonest rights of society, and was therefore manifestly never intended by the organizers of our government. The foreigner, then, has no claim, grounded on the principles of independence, to any participation whatever in any of the privileges of the country. And now, what is the position of a foreigner who prefers such a claim? Precisely the position in which a stranger to your family would be placed, who comes to your door and insists on entering, and making as free with your house and family, and all it contains, as yourself; and on the ground that *all men are created equal.* And what would be a foreigner's chance of obtaining from the American people a claim thus presumptuously preferred? He would have an equal chance with the stranger in the supposed case of your private family. He would probably be dealt with in both cases very much alike. What a sense of justice to your family, and self respect, would prompt you to do as master of your own house in the latter case, it is fair to infer would be done, and would be right to do, in the former.

No. IX.

Claims of the Foreigner to equal rights with Native Citizens, on the ground of abstract natural rights, shown to be groundless.

If the foreigner's claim to *superior* privileges!! over native citizens, is rejected as ridiculous and presumptuous ; if his claims to *equal* privileges, by virtue of the principles of our government, which declare "all men are created equal," are also proved groundless, has he no claim on the ground of his *natural rights* abstractly considered, which being rights by nature are therefore supposed *to take precedence* of any acts of government. This is the only remaining ground on which the slightest shadow of claim can be set up. If I can, therefore, dispose of this, I shall put the foreigner, so far as the argument is concerned, where public opinion will probably ere long, if it has not already, put him, *at the mercy of the* American People *to dispose of as they in their good pleasure shall see fit* ; to admit him into the country on just such condition as they shall be pleased to prescribe, or to refuse him admittance, or to send him out of the country if the safety of the community shall seem to them to require the measure. I would suggest to the memories of my readers the truth that the AMERICAN PEOPLE possess ABSOLUTE SOVEREIGNTY, a truth which seems to be quite forgotten, not alone by the foreigner, but by some who call themselves Americans.

Much is said and written just now of *natural rights*. What is meant by *natural rights?* Strictly they mean the rights belonging to man in a state of nature; that is, in his insulated state, unconnected with any other human being. They are called also *absolute* rights. They are privileges properly belonging to him while *alone*. I find in Chancellor Kent's 24th lecture, this passage, "the absolute rights of individuals may be resolved into the right of personal security, the right of personal liberty, and the right to acquire and enjoy property." This proposition I cannot help thinking is demonstratively illogical, and indefinite. Absolute rights had just been defined, by the same distinguished jurist, to be "such as belong to individuals in a *single, unconnected state*." Let us imagine such an insulated individual; Adam, for example, before another human being was created.—What were his absolute or natural rights? Can they not be condensed into the *single right to make himself as happy as he can, consistent with the laws of his creation;* and if so, what grounds are there for the distinctions, as applied to an *insulated* human being, *right of personal security*, since there is no one to threaten his life; *right of personal liberty*, since there is no one to take it away; or *right to acquire and enjoy property*, since there is no one to dispute his claim to every thing, and any thing in the world? It is clear that these distinctions cannot be logically predicated of man in his *insulated* state.

The natural rights of a man then are properly summed up in a *single right*, that of making himself as happy as he can, consistently with the laws of his creation. This same original natural right to make himself happy belongs to every man individually, but only on the supposition that each individual is entirely separate from all others, that each and every man is a hermit, absolutely cut off from all communication with any other of his species, and shut up in a world of his own. For the moment two or more men are brought on to the same domain, and into society with each other, it is perfectly manifest that every thing in relation to right is completely changed. A *social state* has commenced, *social duties* are introduced, the *selfish principle* inherent in *natural right* is, as a governing principle, banished, the natural right of each to make himself happy, is restricted, as a matter of course, by the equal and similar right of his neighbour; and a new principle must now be introduced as the governing principle, to prevent the conflicting rights of those thus brought together into society, from producing litigation, and the final annihilation, or subjugation of all, but one. Now, what is this principle? It is that of *social compromise*. Each one in society, in order to constitute society, must of necessity surrender his *proper independence*, each one must consent *to yield so much of his natural right to be happy exclusively;* must consent to such an *expansion* of the right to happiness as shall embrace all in that society, whether it be composed of but two individuals, or hundreds of millions; as many, in short, as can consult together, and maintain their united independence. And here, true Democratic government, the government of the people begins, founded on the basis of *social compromise;* a compromise by which the *natural* right of each individual has been mutually restricted to produce the greater blessings of *social* right. If *natural rights* then are now insisted upon, it is evident that they can no longer be demanded in their original *unlimited* sense; they must ever be limited by the restrictions which society by power and authority conceded to it, in its formation, for the purpose of promoting the "greatest happiness of the greatest number for the longest time," has imposed on the original right. In short, *natural right*, which is the right of *the one*, has yielded to *social right*, which is the right of *the many*. Social right is consequently *superior* to natural right, inasmuch as it can justly abridge natural right. This I think is clear; and it is the democratic principle of the right of the *majority* over the *minority*. Let us follow out this principle. As members of society in-

crease, growing up from families, they form into smaller, and then into larger communities, until the whole earth is filled. Now if two or more of these smaller communities combine into a larger community, and can maintain a social existence independent of others, the *social right* of the larger body is superior to, and controls the social right of the smaller bodies within its boundaries. This surrender of a portion of social right on the part of the smaller communities is as necessary to form a larger state, as the surrender of natural right in the first instance, in order to form society at all. So that, as the *natural right* of individuals was yielded in the first instance to social right, so the social right of the smaller communities is in their turn yielded to the superior right of the larger. Thus nations, when justly and naturally formed, have their root in the right of the people to consult their own happiness even on the broadest and most extended scale of society, the majority always controlling, by conceded right, the minority.

Among those larger states into which the world is formed, our Republic, these United States, alone acknowledges this basis of society. It has its distinct, separate place as an independent community, possessing exclusive control within its boundaries of all the interests of the lesser communities of which the whole Republic is composed. It fought and won its battle of independence, and maintains as yet its independent existence. If this reasoning is correct, what becomes of the claim set up by foreigners, and their advocates, to *equal* privileges with native citizens *in this country*. On what principle do they mean to defend it? What are the differences in the circumstances of the native citizen and the foreigner? The *native citizen* is, *by his birth*, a member of this independent community. He was born under its laws, and in the enjoyment of the liberty left by those who won it as a legacy to their children. It is the peculiar birthright of Americans, to have a greater share in the management of their own government than any other people whatever possess in theirs. The *foreigner*, on the contrary *by his birth* belongs to another country, to a separate, independent community. He never has belonged to this Republic in any way. The very question in debate is, how can he become a member of this Republic? He has never had the same rights bestowed upon him in any country, as he acquires in being a citizen in this. What right of admission can he claim? Is it by *natural right?* But natural right is in this country controlled by *social right*. No man here resists successfully the rights of the majority by his individual claim of natural right. And the social rights of the smaller communities are controlled by the superior rights of the larger, and these again by the paramount right of the great state which includes all the others. There is here no place for the claim of the foreigner to admission on any terms into the Republic. Thus we come at last, by the deductions of sound reason, to a conclusion coinciding with the uniform practice of the government from its foundation; the conclusion that the people by the voice of their government may grant permission to enter the country, or withhold permission, and may prescribe their own conditions as they may think *expedient*, and without violating the rights natural or acquired of any human being. To show that these are the principles of the government, I need only quote some of the phrases of the preamble to the Constitution of the United States. "*We, the people* of the United States, in order to form a more perfect union, establish justice, insure *domestic tranquillity*, provide for the *common defence*, promote the *general welfare*, and secure *the blessings of liberty to ourselves* and OUR POSTERITY, *do ordain and establish*," &c. The Declaration of Independence also proclaims kindred sentiments, "To secure these rights, governments are instituted among men, *deriving their just powers from the consent of the governed*. Whenever any form of government becomes destructive of these ends, *it is the right of the people* to alter or to abolish it, and to substitute a new government, laying the foundation on such principles, and organizing its power *in such form, as* TO THEM SHALL SEEM MOST LIKELY TO EFFECT THEIR SAFETY AND HAPPINESS."

The sophistry therefore that would deduce a claim for the foreigner from natural right, is exposed. Neither natural rights, nor social right, nor any other right, nor any legitimate deductions from the principles nor practice of the government give him the slightest claim, even personally to enter upon the territory of the United States, much less to prefer a claim to share in the administration of its affairs. If he comes at all, it is *by permission;* if he stays, it is *by permission;* if he has any privileges in this country, they are granted him *by permission* of the people speaking through their official organs; and this people *can refuse him permission to come, in the first instance, can deny him leave to stay, can temporarily withhold,* or *entirely abolish all privileges granted him, and send him out of the country, can take away his liberty, yes, and even his life,* if they shall judge any of these measures necessary "*to insure domestic tranquillity,*" to provide for the *common defence,* "to promote the *general welfare,* or TO SECURE THE BLESSINGS OF LIBERTY TO OURSELVES AND OUR POSTERITY."

What sound reason sanctions, and the principles of our government sanction, is sanctioned also by common sense. Let me illustrate it by a recurrence to the case of the stranger and your own family.

If a stranger should present himself at your door, and request ever so civilly to become one of the family, you would scarcely be persuaded by any sophistry that you violated any of his *rights natural* or *social,* or of any other character, if you refused his request altogether, at your pleasure; or prescribed to him on what terms he might come, if you acceded to his request; or turned him out of doors, if he behaved himself disorderly, and endangered the comfort or happiness of your family.

No. X.

The injury done to Foreigners by the introduction of Jesuits into the country. The censures upon Foreigners collectively, qualified. Suspicion must nevertheless rest on all. Foreign conspiracy is at work, and its designs must be inquired into, and arrested. The danger is real and imminent. The entrance of Foreigners into the country should be guarded with strong barriers.

IT will doubtless appear to most intelligent Americans, especially those of them who have not been much in contact with the population of our great cities, that I might have spared myself, and my readers, some time in seriously combating the claim of *strangers,* of *foreigners* in the country, to any rights or privileges in it, except such as are granted by the *gracious permission,* (to borrow from abroad an appropriate phrase,) of the *Sovereign* of these United States, namely *the People.* Few, out of the great cities, are aware what sophistry has of late been spread among the more ignorant class of foreigners, to induce them to clan together, and to assert what they are pleased to call their rights. The ridiculous claim to superior privileges over native citizens, which I have noticed, is a specimen; one of many, in which Jesuit sophistry is at work to keep the slaves of superstition and ignorance still bound in their chains. A witty sophism, like the one to which I have alluded, operates on the minds of this degraded multitude with the weight that the most substantial truth possesses upon the intelligent mind. It is proper therefore to draw attention to it for many reasons; one of the most important of which, is to show to the American community, to what dangers they would be exposed, were that general intelligence among the people to become extinct, which is necessary to detect and expose the subtle machinations of Jesuit conspirators. Jesuitism is full of expedients of the kind I have alluded to, and as we have Jesuits avowedly, and systematically, and diligently at work in our society, in the pay and interest of foreign powers, we ought to be watchful of all their movements. There are no greater enemies of the emigrant population than these Holy Alliance emissaries. Already have they done them irreparable injury. Already are witnessed the fruits of their disorganizing efforts. Already has the influence of bad councils led the deluded emigrant, particularly the Irish emigrant, to adopt such a course as to alienate from him the American people. Emigrants have been induced to prefer such arrogant claims, they have nurtured their foreign feelings and their foreign nationality to such a degree, and manifested such a determination to create and strengthen a separate and a foreign interest, that the American people can endure it no longer, and a direct hostile interest is now in array against them. This is an effect natural from such a cause; it is one long ago predicted in the hope of averting the evil. If evil is the consequence, the writer at least washes his hands of the guilt. The name and character of foreigner has, by this conduct of emigrants and their advocates, become odious, and the public voice is becoming louder and louder, and it will increase to unanimity, or at least so far as real American feeling pervades the hearts of Americans, until its language will be intelligible and audible even to those deaf ears, who now affect neither to hear, nor to heed it. When I say that the name of foreigner has become odious, I speak of a fact, not in approval of the fact. No one more than the writer can lament the apparent, (for it is only apparent,) indiscriminate censure of innocent and guilty together, which is unavoidable in combating an evil of this magnitude and character; he has no fears that the severity of any strictures which truth compels him to make upon *foreigners collectively*, will give umbrage to a single intelligent and really naturalized citizen. For such a citizen, if he has been long a citizen, must be fully as conscious as the writer, that the habitual and almost *time-sanctioned* abuses of naturalization, have now reached an important and most dangerous crisis. The naturalized citizen who conducts consistently, who has become an American in reality, and not merely by profession, is not touched by any censure of mine. Neither is the foreigner who is temporarily or officially here; he is professedly an alien, and meddles not, (at least legally,) with our politics. It is that anomalous, nondescript, *hermaphrodite*, Jesuit thing, neither foreigner nor native, yet a moiety of each, now one, now the other, both or neither, as circumstances suit, against whom I war; a naturalized *foreigner*, not a naturalized *citizen;* a man who from Ireland, or France, or Germany, or other foreign lands, renounces his native country and adopts America, professes to become an American, and still, being received and sworn to be a citizen, talks, (for example,) of Ireland as "his home," as "his beloved country," resents any thing said against the Irish as said against him, glories in being Irish, forms and cherishes an Irish interest, brings hither Irish local feuds, and forgets, in short, all his new obligations as an American, and retains both a name and a feeling and a practice in regard to his adopted country at war with propriety, with decency, with gratitude, and with true patriotism. I hold no parley with such contradictions as Irish fellow-citizens, French fellow-citizens, or German fellow-citizens. With as much consistency might we say *foreign natives*, or *hostile friends*. But the present is no time either for compliment or nice discrimination. When the country is invaded by an army, it is not the moment to indulge in pity towards the deluded soldiers of the various hostile corps, who act as they are commanded by their superior officers. It is then no time to make distinctions among the officers, lest we injure those who are involuntarily fighting against us, or who may be friends in the enemy's camp. The first thing is to bring the whole army to unconditional surrender, and when they have laid down their arms in a body, and acknowledged our sovereignty, then good fellowship, and courtesy, and pity will have leisure to indulge in discriminating friends from foes, and in showing to each their respective and appropriate sympathies.

We have now to resist the *momentous* evil that threatens us from *Foreign Conspiracy*. The *Conspirators* are in the *foreign importations*. Innocent and guilty are brought over together. We must of necessity suspect them all. That we are most seriously endangered, admits not of the slightest doubt; we are experiencing the natural reaction of European upon American principles, and it is infatuation, it is madness not to see it, not to guard against it. A subtle attack is making upon us by foreign powers. The proofs are as strong as the nature of the case allows. They have been adduced again and again, and they have not only been uncontradicted, but silently acquiesced in, and have acquired fresh confirmation by every day's observation. The arbitrary governments of Europe,—those governments who keep the people in the most abject obedience at the point of the bayonet, with Austria at their head, have combined to attack us in every vulnerable point that the nation exposes to their assault. They are impelled by self-preservation to attempt our destruction,—they must destroy democracy. It is with them a case of life and death,—they must succeed or perish. If they do not overthrow American liberty, American liberty will overthrow their despotism. They know this fact well. They have declared it. They are acting in accordance with their convictions, and declarations, and they are acting wisely. They have already sent their chains, and oh! to our shame be it spoken, are fastening them upon a *sleeping* victim. Americans, you are marked for their prey, not by foreign bayonets, but *by weapons surer of effecting the conquest of liberty* than all the munitions of physical combat in the military or naval storehouses of Europe. Will you not awake to the apprehension of the reality and extent of your danger? Will you be longer deceived by the pensioned Jesuits, who having surrounded your press, are now using it all over the country to stifle the cries of danger, and lull your fears by attributing your alarm to a false cause. Up! up! I beseech you. Awake! To your posts! Let the tocsin sound from Maine to Louisiana. Fly to protect the vulnerable places of your Constitution and Laws. Place your guards; you will need them, and quickly too.—And first, shut your gates. Shut the open gates. The very first step of safety is here. It is the beginning of defence. Your enemies, in the guise of friends, by thousands, are at this moment rushing in to your ruin through the open portals of *naturalization*. Stop them, or you are lost, irrevocably lost. The first battle is here at the gates. Concentrate here. And be sure your enemy will here show his strength; you here can test his force or his existence, if you indeed doubt his existence. He will dispute this entrance inch by inch. Already is he alarmed, already has he set in motion his troops to resist. Will you despise the cry of danger? Well, be it so. Believe the foreign Jesuit rather than your own countrymen. Open wide your doors. Yes, throw down your walls. Invite, nay allure, your enemies. Enlarge your alms-houses and your prisons; be not sparing of your money; complain not of the outrages in your streets, nor the burden of your taxes. You will be repaid in praises of your toleration and liberality. What though European despots have compelled you to be the nurses of their halt, and blind, and naked, and the keepers of their criminals; what though they have compelled you to the necessity of employing your lives in toiling and providing for their outcast poor, and have caused you to be vexed, and your habits outraged by the expatriated turbulence of their cities, instead of allowing you to rejoice in the prosperity, and happiness, and peaceful neighbourhood of your own well-provided, well-instructed children.

Have you no reward? Oh, yes; your country is filling with a noble foreign population, all friends of liberty, all undoubted Democrats, taught in the school of Democratic Europe, accustomed to huzza with one voice for liberty, and under the guidance of Jesuit leaders well trained; far famed, long tried friends of Democracy; and to make assurance doubly sure, selected with the greatest care by Austria's Democratic Emperor, and Rome's Democratic Pope, who watch them with jealous eyes, and if not faithful in *upholding Democracy*, will deprive them of their stipulated wages, and recall them home, to receive their merited punishment—an Archbishop's see, or a Cardinal's hat. Democracy is safe with such keepers. The country is in no danger. Sleep on.

No. XI.

The imperious necessity of a change in the Naturalization Laws.—The dangers from the alarming increase and present character of foreign immigration.—The political changes in Europe double the dangers to the country from foreign immigration.—The test of the existence and strength of the conspiracy in the country, and the first step in the defence against it.

The propriety, nay, the imperious necessity of a change in the Naturalization Laws, is the point to which it is indispensable to the safety of the country, that the attention of Americans, as a whole people, should at this moment be concentrated. It is a national question, not only separate from, but *superior* to all others. All other questions which divide the nation, are peculiarly of a domestic character; they relate to matters between American and American. Whether the *bank system* is, or is not, adverse to our democratic institutions; whether *internal improvement* is constitutionally intrusted to the management of the general government, or reserved to the states respectively; whether *monopolies* of any kind are just or unjust; whether the *right of instructing* representatives is to be allowed or resisted; whether *the high offices* of the nation are safest administered by these or by those citizens; all these, and many kindred questions, are entirely of a domestic character, to be settled between ourselves, in the just democratic mode, by majority, by the prevailing voice of the American people declared through the *ballot box*. But the question of *naturalization*, the question whether *foreigners, not yet arrived*, shall or shall not be admitted to the American right of balloting, is a matter in which the American people are in a certain sense, on one side as the original and exclusive possessors of the privilege, and foreigners on the other, as petitioners for a participation in that privilege; for the privilege of expressing their opinion upon, and assisting to decide all the other questions I have enumerated. It is, therefore, a question separate and *superior* to all these. It is a fundamental question; it affects the very foundation of our institutions, it bears directly and vitally on the *principle of the ballot* itself, that principle which decides the gravest questions of policy among Americans, nay, which can decide the very existence of the government, or can change its form at any moment. And surely this vital principle is amply protected from injury? To secure this point, every means which a people jealous of their liberties could devise was doubtless gathered about it for its preservation? It is not guarded. Be astonished, Americans, at the oversight! The mere statement of the provisions of the Naturalization Law, is sufficient, one would think, to startle any American who reflects at all. FIVE YEARS' RESIDENCE GIVES THE FOREIGNER, WHATEVER BE HIS CONDITION OR CHARACTER, THIS MOST SACRED PRIVILEGE OF ASSISTING TO CONTROL, AND ACTUALLY OF CONTROLLING (*there is not a guard to prevent*,) ALL THE DOMESTIC INTERESTS OF AMERICA. A simple *five years' residence*, allows any foreigner, (no matter what his character, whether friend or enemy of freedom, whether an exile from proscription, or a pensioned Jesuit, commissioned to serve the interests of Imperial Despots,) to handle this "*lock of our strength.*" How came it to pass? How is it possible that so vital a point as the ballot box was not constitutionally surrounded with double, ay, with treble guards? How is it that this *heart* of Democracy was left so exposed; yes; this very *heart* of the body politic, in which, in periodical pulsations, the opinions of the people meet, to go forth again as law to the extremities of the nation; this *heart* left so absolutely without protection, that the murderous eye of Imperial Despots across the deep, can, not only watch it in all its movements, but they are invited from its very nakedness, to reach out their hands to stab it. The figure is not too strong; their blow is aimed, now, whilst I write, at this very heart of our institutions. How is it that none of our sagacious statesmen foresaw this danger to the republic through the unprotected ballot box? It was foreseen. It did not escape the prophetic eye of Jefferson. He foresaw, and from the beginning foretold the evil, and uttered his warning voice. *Mr. Jefferson denounced the encouragement of emigration.* And, oh! consistency, where is thy blush? he who is now urging

Jefferson's own recommendation on this vital point, is condemned by some who call themselves Jeffersonian democrats ; by some journalists who in one column profess Jeffersonian principles, while in the next they denounce both the principles and the policy of Jefferson, and (with what semblance of consistency let them show if they can,) defend a great political evil, against which Jefferson left his written protest. It may be convenient, for purposes best known to themselves, for such journalists to desert their democratic principles, while loudly professing still to hold them ; but the people, who are neither blind nor deaf, will soon perceive whose course is most consistent with that great apostle of democratic liberty. Do they ask, would you defend Mr. Jefferson's opinions when they are wrong?— I answer, prove them to be wrong, and I will desert them. Truth and justice are superior to all men. I advocate Jefferson's opinions, not because they are Jefferson's, but because his opinions are in accordance with truth and sound policy.— Let me show that Mr. Jefferson's opinions in relation to emigration are proved by experience to be sound.

What were the circumstances of the country when laws so favourable to the foreigner were passed to induce him to emigrate and settle in this country? The answer is obvious. Our early history explains it. In our national infancy we needed the strength of *numbers*. Powerful nations, to whom we were accessible by fleets, and consequently also by armies, threatened us. Our land had been the theatre of contests between French, and English, and Spanish armies, for more than a century. Our numbers were so few and so scattered, that as a people we could not unite to repel aggression. The war of Independence, too, had wasted us. We wanted *numerical strength;* we felt our weakness in numbers. *Safety,* then, national *safety,* was the motive which urged us to use every effort to increase our population, and to inducea foreign emigration. Then foreigners seemed all-important, and the policy of alluring them hither, too palpable to be opposed successfully even by the remonstrances of Jefferson. We could be benefited by the emigrants, and we in return could bestow on them a gift beyond price, by simply making them citizens. Manifest as this advantage seemed in the increase of our numerical strength, Mr. Jefferson looked beyond the advantage of the moment, and saw the distant evil. His reasoning, already quoted in a former number, will bear to be repeated. "I beg leave," says Mr. Jefferson, "to propose a doubt. The present desire of America is to produce rapid population by as great importations of foreigners as possible. But is this founded in good policy? *The advantage proposed, is the multiplication of numbers.* But are there no inconveniences to be thrown into the scale against the advantage expected from a multiplication of numbers by the importation of foreigners? It is for the happiness of those united in society to harmonize as much as possible in matters which they must of necessity transact together."

"Civil government being the sole object of forming societies, its administration must be conducted by common consent. Every species of government has its specific principles. Ours, perhaps, are more peculiar than those of any other in the universe. It is a composition of the freest principles of the English constitution, with others derived from natural right and natural reason. To these nothing can be more opposed than the maxims of absolute monarchies. Yet, from such, we are to expect the greatest number of emigrants. *They will bring with them the principles of the governments they leave, imbibed in their early youth ; or, if able to throw them off, it will be in exchange for an unbounded licentiousness,* passing, as is usual, from one extreme to another. It would be a miracle were they to stop precisely at the point of temperate liberty. These principles, with their language, they will transmit to their children. *In proportion to their numbers, they will share with us the legislation. They will infuse into it their spirit, warp and bias its directions, and render it a heterogeneous, incoherent, distracted mass.*"

"I may appeal to experience, for a verification of these conjectures. But, if they be not *certain in event,* are they not *possible, are they not probable?* Is it not safer to wait with patience—for the attainment of any degree of population desired or expected? May not our government be more homogeneous, more peaceable, more durable?" He asks, what would be the condition of France if twenty millions of Americans were suddenly imported into that kingdom? and adds—"If it would be *more turbulent*, less happy, less strong, we may believe that the addition of *half a million of foreigners* would produce a *similar effect here*. If they come of themselves, they are entitled to all the rights of citizenship; *but I doubt the expediency of inviting them by extraordinary encouragements*." Now, if under the most favourable circumstances for the country, when it could most be benefited, when numbers were most urgently needed, Mr. Jefferson could discover the evil afar off, and protest against encouraging foreign immigration, how much more is the measure now to be deprecated, when circumstances have so entirely changed, that instead of *adding strength* to the country, immigration *adds weakness*, weakness physical and moral! And what overwhelming force does Mr. Jefferson's reasoning acquire, by the vast change of circumstances which has taken place both in Europe and in this country, in our earlier and in our later condition.—*Then* we were few, feeble, and scattered. *Now* we are numerous, strong, and concentrated. *Then* our accessions by immigration were real accessions of strength from the ranks of the learned and the good, from the enlightened mechanic and artisan, and intelligent husbandman. *Now* immigration is the accession of weakness, from the ignorant and the vicious, or the priest-ridden slaves of Ireland and Germany, or the outcast tenants of the poorhouses and prisons of Europe. And again. *Then* our beautiful system of government had not been unfolded to the world to the terror of tyrants; the rising brightness of American Democracy was not yet so far above the horizon as to wake their slumbering anxieties, or more than to gleam faintly, in hope, upon their enslaved subjects. *Then* emigration was natural, it was an attraction of affinities, it was an attraction of liberty to liberty. Emigrants were the proscribed for conscience' sake, and for opinion's sake, the real lovers of liberty, Europe's loss, and our gain.

Now American Democracy is denounced by name by foreign despots, waked with its increasing brilliancy. Its splendour dazzles them. It alarms them, for it shows their slaves their chains. And it must be extinguished. *Now* emigration is changed; naturalization has become the door of entrance not alone to the ever welcome lovers of liberty, but also for the priest-ridden troops of the Holy Alliance, with their Jesuit officers well skilled in all the arts of darkness. Now emigrants are selected for a service to their tyrants, and by their tyrants; not for their affinity to liberty, but for their mental servitude, and their docility in obeying the orders of their priests. They are transported in thousands, nay, in *hundreds of thousands*, to our shores, to our loss and Europe's gain.

It may be, Americans, that you still doubt the *existence* of a conspiracy, and the reality of danger from Foreign Combination; or, if the attempt is made, you yet doubt the *power* of any such secret intrigue in your society. Do you wish to test its existence and its power? It is easy to apply the test. *Test it by attempting a change in the Naturalization Law.* Take the ground that such a change must be made, that *no foreigner who comes into the country after the law is passed shall ever be allowed the right of suffrage*. Stand firmly to this single point, and you will soon discover where the enemy is, and the tactics he employs. This is the spear of Ithuriel. Apply its point. You will find your enemy, though now squat like a toad fast by the ear of our confidence, suddenly roused to show his infernal origin.

Look a moment at the proposition. You will perceive that in its very nature there is nothing to excite the opposition of a single citizen, native or naturalized, in the whole country, *provided*, be it distincly borne in mind, *that he is not implicated in the conspiracy*. This prohibition, in the proposed change of the law, it is evident, touches not in any way the *native American*, neither does it touch in the slightest degree the already granted privileges of the *naturalized citizen*, nor the *foreigner now in the country*, who is waiting to be naturalized, nor even *the foreigner on his way hither;* no, *not an individual* in the whole country is unfavourably affected by the provisions of such a law, not an individual *except alone the foreign Jesuit, the Austrian stipendiary with his intriguing myrmidons.* And how is he affected by it? He is deprived of his *passive obedience* forces; he can no longer use his power over his slaves, *to interfere in our political concerns;* he can no longer use them in his Austrian master's service; and he therefore, be assured, will resist with all the desperation of a detected brigand. He will raise an outcry. He will fill the public ear with cries of *intolerance.* He will call the measure religious bigotry, and illiberality, and religious persecution, and other popular catchwords, to deceive the unreflecting ear. But, be not deceived; when you hear him, set your mark upon him. That is the man. Try then this test. Again, I say, let the proposition be that the law of the land be so changed, that NO FOREIGNER WHO COMES INTO THE COUNTRY AFTER THE LAW IS PASSED SHALL EVER BE ENTITLED TO THE RIGHT OF SUFFRAGE. This is just ground; it is practicable ground; it is defensible ground, and it is safe and prudent ground; and I cannot better close than in the words of Mr. Jefferson: "The time to guard against corruption and tyranny is *before* they shall have gotten hold on us; IT IS BETTER TO KEEP THE WOLF OUT OF THE FOLD, THAN TO TRUST TO DRAWING HIS TEETH AND TALONS AFTER HE HAS ENTERED."

APPENDIX.

Note (1.) page 16.

This organization of foreigners, to act upon our institutions, not only formed in foreign countries, but even within our own borders, is indeed a very serious matter. Why are the people so blind to the danger which threatens them from this source? What reason can be assigned, why they who profess to have become Americans, should organize themselves into Foreign National Societies all over the country; and under their foreign appellation, hold correspondence with each other to promote their foreign interest? Can any good reason be given why such *foreign associations* should be allowed to exist in this country? The Irish have been thus organized for many years. The objects of *one* of these Irish societies will serve to illustrate the objects generally of all these associations in the midst of us. "*The Boston Hibernian Lyceum*," says the Catholic Diary of March 14, 1835, "organized about *two years* ago, is composed of *Irish young men*, for the diffusion among each other—of what?—of MUTUAL SYMPATHY and MUTUAL CO-OPERATION, in whatever may aid to qualify them to *meet and discharge their* RESPONSIBILITIES as THE REPRESENTATIVES OF THEIR NATIVE, as well as citizens of their adopted, COUNTRY, as IRISHMEN and Americans." Here we have an avowal directly of an organization to promote a foreign interest in this country! Similar organizations, in correspondence with each other, have been made for years without attracting attention until within a few months. They have now become a subject of very serious consideration. The Jesuits have taken the alarm, and are casting about for a plausible excuse to offer for these organizations. What excuse can they offer? Was it for defence? Against whom? Was it for attack? Whom were they going to fight? Whom had they reason to fear? A Jesuit, in the Baltimore American, is preparing the way to bring forth a grand excuse, presuming on the slumbering fears, or the indifference, or ignorance of the community. I will therefore endeavour to anticipate him. Hear what he says: "*Hundreds of thousands* of Roman Catholics are *annually* pouring into our country." Take notice, in passing, of the numbers pouring into the country, "*Hundreds of thousands, annually!*" "They are spread over the fertile valley;—leave them unmolested, and they are merged in the great mass of the community,—but persecute them, *receive them with jealousy and avowed distrust*—insult them—drive them to the wall—*put them upon their defence*, and we may indeed fear an '*organization*'—they MUST AND WILL ORGANIZE—*they will organize*, for all that life is dear—*they will organize*, for all that eternity has to offer," &c.

Now here are threats thrown out that these foreigners, (by hundreds of thousands too,) *will organize;* that they MUST AND WILL ORGANIZE. And why? Because jealousy and distrust has been excited in the minds of Americans, not for fear that they should organize, but on account of their having ALREADY organized; they are going to organize, because they are put on their defence for having organized, and are asked, why have you already organized? As well might they say that the determination to destroy the Convent at Charlestown on the 11th of August by a mob was the cause of the *mysterious provocatives to that mob* which occurred in the Convent a *week or two before*, or that its final destruction was the cause of the threat made *the day before the event* by the Lady Superior that 10,000 Irishmen under the influence of the Bishop, might tear down the houses in Charlestown if the Convent were injured. All these will be true when *effects* precede their *cause*.

To question their principles, civil or religious, it seems is "*to persecute them;*" to doubt their fitness to manage the political concerns of the republic, is "*to insult them;*" to prefer managing our domestic affairs ourselves, is "*to drive them to the wall.*" And so these foreigners threaten an organization by hundreds of thousands, to seize by force those privileges of which we may find it necessary to deprive them, and they mean to fight "*for all that life is dear,—for all that eternity has to offer.*" Are Americans prepared to yield to these arrogant airs?

It is notorious that the excitement respecting the Roman Catholic emigrants, has existed scarcely a year. The exposure of foreign designs through the Roman Catholic religion, and the discussions arising out of it, all the riotous conduct of Catholics and others, and among other things the public notice of these very *organizations*, have all occurred *within the last year.*—But the organizations of the Catholics, and particularly of the Irish are of *many years* standing. The

Society at Boston above quoted, and one of the most recent, was formed long before any excitement on the subject "*two years ago*," says the Catholic Diary. It was, discovering these organizations *already formed* on the part of foreigners, that excited the *jealousy and distrust* on the part of the American people, and when the people now "*put these foreigners on their defence*" for these outrages, and ask them what they mean by these suspicious doings; why they conduct in a way to excite jealousy and distrust? They are to be gravely told, we organized ourselves for our protection *yesterday*, in consequence of your *jealousy and distrust* of that organization manifested *to-day;* and your "putting us on our defence," asking us *this day* the meaning of our conduct, is the cause of our forming, *two years ago*, an association to protect ourselves against you!!

This is in truth the argument that is preparing, and unless the people are on their guard, too, and fix in their minds the *order and time of these events*, the Jesuits will succeed in making them believe that all the suspicious organizations of foreigners throughout the land, which have *already existed for several years*, are but of recent origin, forced upon them by what they call persecution, and are lately formed, purely from necessity, for self-defence; and thus they can continue their traitorous associations, under the plea of necessity, and at the same time can show up the American character, as persecuting, and intolerant. Americans, you have Jesuits among you. Of this fact you know there is no doubt; and Jesuits are not idle. Open your eyes, and you will see their workings in almost every day's transactions. You can perceive their dallyings with the press; for by means of facilities which its freedom presents, especially in *anonymous* writing, and by their organized concert throughout the country, they can easily give a *distorted appearance to public opinion.* Of this you should be constantly aware. They will of course write under the guise of protestants and republicans. The wolf does not come as a wolf, but as one of the fold. Watch them. You cannot mistake, in receiving Jesuits with "*jealousy and distrust.*" They will yet give you trouble.

What has the Roman Catholic system to do with politics?

Let me show the connexion. I have said that we are compelled to examine the nature of the Roman Catholic system. We cannot avoid it. It is forced upon our notice, by the fact that foreign governments, hostile to our institutions, are combined together expressly to spread it through this country. If the people are satisfied of this single truth, *of the existence of the St. Leopold Foundation*, let me ask, how ought they to view its object? Here is an extensive combination of *arbitrary sovereigns*, with Austria at their head, organized in a Society; levying contributions, by means of all the ecclesiastical and civil officers of a territory of an extent containing more than 23,000,000 of inhabitants, and employing as its agents the famous order of *Jesuits*, and for the purpose of spreading the Roman Catholic religion through the United States. Nay, more; this society is but one of *three*, at least. There is one in Italy, and another in France, organized for the same purpose. There is no mistake here. No one, not even the Jesuits have pretended to deny this fact. And is it really of no consequence to know what this system is, to spread which, over this whole country, the most deadly enemies of Democracy abroad are employing such extensive and powerful associations? Is it in character with a true sentinel of freedom, when he knows such a fact as this, instead of giving the alarm, to cry *no danger; all's well?* Or is he a guardian of the public safety who, when the sentinel challenges the suspicious looking intruders, cries out against him, *Persecution;* and clears the way for their free entrance into the city?

What is the system that Austria and the other despots of Europe are so vigorously promoting in these United States? It is Popery. What is the character of Popery? 'You must not ask that question,' says one. 'You have no right to ask it.' 'It is persecuting the Catholics to make so rude an inquiry.' 'Every man has a right to his religion,' says another. 'No Church and State cries a third.' 'The Catholics are as good as the Presbyterians any day,' says a fourth. 'It is the oldest religion, and therefore is the best,' says a fifth. 'It is *persecution*, and *intolerance*, and *illiberality*, and *bigotry*,' cries a sixth, 'for the Roman Catholic religion is changed; it is not that bloody, persecuting religion that it was in by-gone times, when John Huss and others were burnt as heretics. Roman Catholics have grown tolerant and liberal; they are now favourable to liberty; they advocate all the rights of man, such as, right of private judgment; the liberty of the press. They have imbibed the spirit of the age.' These, and such as these, are the popular and set answers when the question is asked, what is the character of Popery? The last is the only answer worth a moment's attention. For it seems to have more of the *anodyne* in it than any of the others. If the Roman Catholic religion is essentially changed in its objectionable features; if it has got rid of its arbitrary principles, and become democratic; if it is become tolerant and liberal; if it now inculcates truth and integrity, instead of falsehood, and fraud, I admit that much of its objectionable character, at least politically speaking, is removed. Yet, who says it is changed?

Will any Roman Catholic Bishop say it has changed any of its principles one iota? No, they have never said it officially, and never will. But even if it were true, the fact that European despots are forcing it upon us, would, in spite of all, throw a suspicious complexion over it. But now, suppose that this Roman Catholic religion, instead of being changed in its objectionable features, *still* avowedly *rigidly adheres to its most obnoxious and arbitrary principles;* that, instead of being democratic in character, it is the perfect opposite of democracy; that, instead of being tolerant and liberal, and conciliating, it is *intolerant*, and *illiberal*, and *denunciatory;* that, instead of being *in favour* of the liberty of the press, and *allowing* the right of private judgment, it *denounces* these rights; that, instead of inculcating truth and strict integrity, *it teaches the practice of falsehood* and *fraud*. Ah! you will say, that is a different affair. If such a character could be fixed upon the Roman Catholic system, and this system is that which is now patronized by the monarchs of Europe to be propagated by Jesuits through this country, it becomes truly a serious matter, and we must inquire into it.—And is there any Roman Catholic ecclesiastic who, *authorized by his superior*, will dare to deny, under his own proper name,

1st. That the Roman Catholic priesthood are taught at this day, (A. D. 1835,) to account *Protestants* worse than *Pagans*.

2d. That they are taught to consider all who are *baptized*, *even by those they term heretics*, as lawfully under the *power of the Church of Rome*, over whom the *Pope has rightful domination*.

3d. That they are taught, that they cannot tolerate the *rites of any* who are not in the church of Rome, and that whenever it is for the good of the church, *they must exterminate them*.

4th. That they are taught, that they may compel, by *corporeal punishments*, all who are baptized; and consequently nearly all, if not all of every Protestant religious denomination to *submit to the Roman church*.

5th. That they are taught that these punishments may be, CONFISCATION OF PROPERTY, EXILE, IMPRISONMENT, and DEATH! ☞

6th. That they are taught, that *expediency alone* may restrain them from the exercise of any of these rights of compulsion against heretics; and that consequently, whenever they have the *power*, and it shall be thought *expedient*, it is their *duty* to exercise them.

Are these startling propositions? Consider them well, Americans. If any Roman Catholic ecclesiastic, any Bishop, or any one authorized by a Bishop, will maintain under his own proper name the *negative* of these six propositions, the writer pledges himself to maintain the *affirmative* under his own proper name. These are the doctrines *now* of the church of Rome.